CULTURE IN ACTION

Graffiti

Jane Bingham

Chicago, Illinois

www.heinemannraintree.com
Visit our website to find out more information about Heinemann-Raintree books.

To order:
☎ Phone 888-454-2279
🖥 Visit www.heinemannraintree.com to browse our catalog and order online.

Edited by Louise Galpine and Rachel Howells
Designed by Kimberly Miracle and Betsy Wernert
Original illustrations © Capstone Global Library Ltd.
Illustrated by kja-artists.com
Picture research by Mica Brancic and Kay Altwegg
Production by Alison Parsons
Originated by Steve Walker, Capstone Global Library Ltd
Printed in China by Leo Paper Products Ltd

13 12 11 10 09
10 9 8 7 6 5 4 3 2 1

Library of Congress Cataloging-in-Publication Data
Bingham, Jane.
  Graffiti / Jane Bingham.
    p. cm. -- (Culture in action)
  Includes bibliographical references and index.
  ISBN 978-1-4109-3401-7 (hc) -- ISBN 978-1-4109-3418-5 (pb) 1. Graffiti--Juvenile literature. 2. Mural painting and decoration--Juvenile literature. I. Title.
  GT3912.B56 2009
  751.7'3--dc22
                    2008054323

Acknowledgments

The author and publishers are grateful to the following for permission to reproduce copyright material: Alamy pp. 6 (Eddie Gerald), **7 bottom** (Tony Watson), 8 (© David Wheeldon), 15 (Tony Lilley), 19 (Darrin Jenkins), 20 (Stock Italia), 25 (Michael Klinec), 26 (EuroStyle Graphics); Corbis p. **16** (Adam Woolfitt); Corbis SYGMA p. 18 (Julio Donoso); Getty Images pp. **5** (Paul Hawthorne), **17 bottom** (AFP/Aris Messinis), 22 (AFP/Timothy A. Clary), 27 (Scott Barbour); iStockphoto 14 (© Michael Valdez), **17 top** (Terraxplorer); Photofusion pp. 12 (Janine Wiedel), 24 (© Colin Edwards); Shutterstock pp. 4 (© Sam Cornwell), 7 top (© Dubassy), 9 (© Stuart Weston), 11 (© Tyler Boyes).

Icon and banner images supplied by Shutterstock: © Alexander Lukin, © ornitopter, © Colorlife, and © David S. Rose.

Cover photograph of student volunteers painting legal graffiti in preparation for the 2008 Olympics in Beijing, China, reproduced with permission of Corbis (epa/Michael Reynolds).

We would like to thank Susie Hodge, Jackie Murphy, and Nancy Harris for their invaluable help in the preparation of this book.

Every effort has been made to contact copyright holders of material reproduced in this book. Any omissions will be rectified in subsequent printings if notice is given to the publishers.

Contents

Important note:

It is fine to draw "graffiti style" designs on paper or in special places where you have permission. But you should NEVER paint or draw on other people's property without permission.

Some words are printed in bold, **like this**. You can find out what they mean by looking in the glossary on page 30.

What Is Graffiti?

Graffiti is the name given to writing, designs, and pictures on walls or other surfaces. It is often done without permission, although there are some places where graffiti is allowed.

Even though writing on public and private property is against the **law**, people still do it. People have been creating graffiti for thousands of years.

An ancient name

The word *graffiti* comes from the Greek word for "writing." People who paint graffiti are usually known as "graffiti writers."

Sometimes, a run-down city street can become covered with graffiti.

Scratches and spray paint

Graffiti comes in several different forms. Sometimes people scratch initials, words, or designs into a surface. Often graffiti is painted, using a paintbrush or a can of spray paint.

Today, most graffiti writers use spray paints to create colorful effects. Spray paints can be used to create freehand designs or **stencil graffiti** (see page 19). Some graffiti writers use thick markers to achieve quick results.

Art or crime?

Many people see graffiti as a crime. They claim it destroys the environment of our towns and cities. Others think graffiti can look good—and even see it as a form of art. What do you think about graffiti?

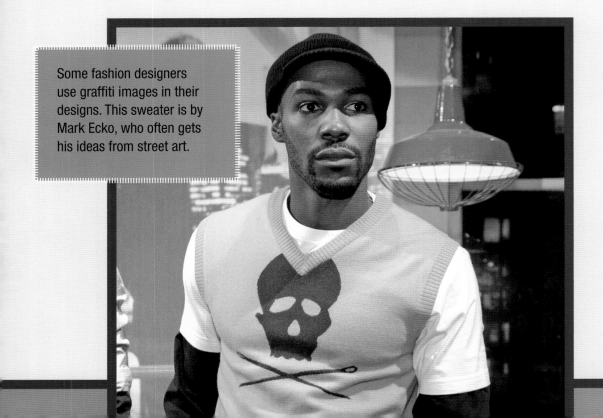

Some fashion designers use graffiti images in their designs. This sweater is by Mark Ecko, who often gets his ideas from street art.

Why Create Graffiti?

What is it that makes someone write on walls and other surfaces? There are several reasons why people decide to make their mark on their environment.

"I was here"

Graffiti is a way of showing that you have been in a certain place. Prisoners locked in dungeons, students sitting at a desk, and tourists visiting a distant monument have all felt the urge to leave some evidence that they were there.

In the past, people simply wrote their name. Others shortened their name to initials, which are quicker and easier to carve or write. Sometimes they added the date as well. Today, most graffiti writers use a short nickname, known as a **tag**.

Painting the Berlin Wall

From 1961 to 1989, the city of Berlin was divided by a famous wall. On one side was East Berlin and on the other was West Berlin. East Berlin was part of East Germany, a **communist** society where everyone was supposed to be equal. People were not allowed to cross the wall. West Berliners protested by covering the wall with graffiti.

This is a section of the Berlin Wall that once divided Berlin in two.

A tag shows that a graffiti writer has visited a place. Writers try to get their tags in as many places as possible.

Something to say

Some people use graffiti to express their views. Writing a message in a public place is a way to state your point of view. This kind of graffiti is created so it is easily seen. It is usually painted in large capital letters.

This graffiti piece is by the British artist Banksy. It makes the point that people are being filmed by security cameras.

Types and Styles

Today's graffiti writers use a range of styles. Some simple graffiti can be created quickly. Other pieces have a lot of patterns and colors and take many hours to complete.

Tags

The most basic element in graffiti is the **tag**. In its simplest form, it is a kind of signature created with spray paint or markers. Having a tag helps **illegal** writers avoid punishment. When they use a tag, their real name can remain unknown.

Throw-ups

When graffiti writers want to paint a bolder version of their tag, they create a "throw-up." These strong designs are quick and easy to "throw up" on a wall. Writers first paint the letter outlines of their tag. Then they fill in the outlines with a different colored paint. Most throw-ups use two strongly contrasting colors, such as red and blue, or silver and black.

Throw-ups are sometimes known as "fills" or "dubs." Dubs is short for "double colors."

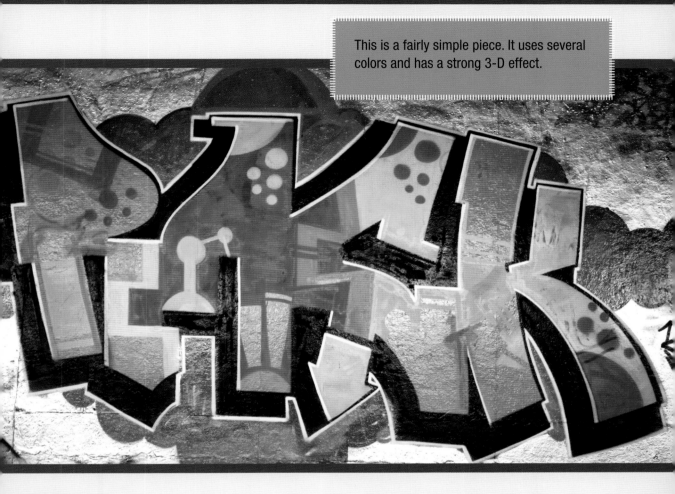

This is a fairly simple piece. It uses several colors and has a strong 3-D effect.

Pieces

A piece is an elaborate version of the artist's tag. The word "piece" comes from "masterpiece." The letters in a piece are first outlined and then filled in, using three or more colors. Pieces use fancy lettering styles (see pages 10–11). They often include **3-D** effects, so the letters seem to stand out from the wall.

Penguin graffiti

The graffiti artist Banksy once painted a message at the London Zoo. He climbed into the penguin **enclosure** and wrote in very large letters: "We're bored of fish."

Straights

The simplest letters used in graffiti are block capitals, also known as **straights**. Straights are usually painted in just two colors, one for the outline and one for the fill. Occasionally, a third color is added to give a 3-D effect.

Bubbles

Bubble letters are rounded versions of ordinary letters. They have curvy outlines so they fit snugly into one another. Because bubble letters are so wide, they provide a great surface for **color fades** (two colors merged gradually into each other).

Write your name in bubble letters

First write your name in capital letters. Then draw around each letter to create bubble letters. Make each letter overlap the one behind. When you are happy with your name, erase the first marks you made and give the letters a two-color fade and a strong black outline.

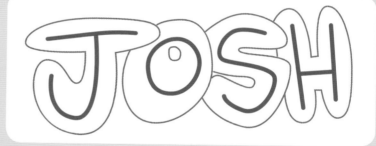

Wildstyle

Wildstyle lettering is the hardest to create. The letters have sharp outlines and they all fit tightly together, like a complicated jigsaw puzzle. Wildstyle pieces often feature arrows pointing in different directions. Wildstyle lettering is created as a work of art, rather than just as words.

Characters

Some graffiti pieces include a cartoon character, either inside the letters or beside the piece. Graffiti writers create their own characters, but cartoon monsters and aliens are popular.

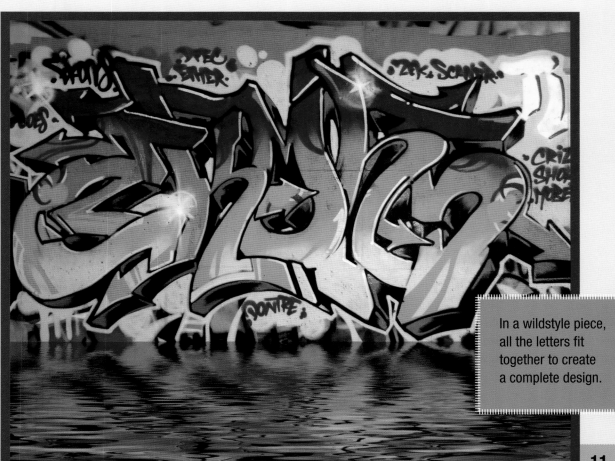

In a wildstyle piece, all the letters fit together to create a complete design.

11

The wall of this community youth center has graffiti on the subject of sport.

Productions

Some graffiti writers create large-scale **murals**, called productions. Productions combine several pieces and characters. They are often made by a group of graffiti writers working together.

Productions usually have a single-color background. They often have a theme, such as "under the sea" or "out in space."

Animal tags

Graffiti writers often choose a tag that shows something about them. Can you think of an animal tag that reflects your personality? Are you a tiger, a turtle, or a rhino? When you have decided on an animal, you are ready to create your tag.

Steps to follow:

1. Practice writing your animal tag in graffiti style. (It helps if your animal name is not too long!) You can use bubble letters or straights.

2. Choose two or more colors for your tag. Practice using your colors for outlines, fills, and color fades.

3. When you are happy with your tag, draw a small cartoon character of your animal. It can be a face or a whole animal, but keep it really simple.

4. Now put your tag and your character together, stand back, and admire your piece!

You can also combine several pieces and characters to make a production with an animal theme.

A Very Long History

When did graffiti begin? Some people claim that **prehistoric** rock art is the earliest form of graffiti. They give examples of cave paintings dating back 30,000 years. Other people think that graffiti began soon after humans learned to write, around 5,000 years ago. No matter when it started, there is no doubt that graffiti has a very long history.

Ancient writings

Messages and names have been found on the walls of buildings from ancient Egypt, Greece, and Rome. In North America, carvings survive on the stones of Mayan temples in Mexico that date from around 400 BCE, about 2,400 years ago.

This ancient graffiti was found in rocks in the Nevada Desert. It dates from around 10,000 years ago.

These examples of Roman graffiti were found in the buried city of Pompeii, Italy. They have survived for almost 2,000 years.

Roman records

The best examples of early graffiti come from the ancient Roman city of Pompeii in Italy. In 79 CE (around 1,900 years ago), Pompeii was completely buried in ash when a nearby volcano erupted. Hundreds of years later, **archaeologists** (people who learn about the past) uncovered the city. They found many walls carved with Roman graffiti.

The people of Pompeii carved messages of love, curses on their enemies, and magic spells. The Roman graffiti included quotes from famous writers and cartoon drawings of local **politicians**.

Stupid scribblers

"I wonder, O wall, that you have not fallen in ruins from supporting the stupidities of so many scribblers."

—Roman graffiti on a wall in Pompeii

Medieval marks

Many examples of graffiti have survived from the **medieval** (1000–1450 CE) period. Prisoners in dungeons scratched their names and the dates they were there. Some even wrote last messages before they died. Medieval builders carved special signs, known as masons' marks, into the beams and walls of buildings where they were working.

Travelers and soldiers

By the 1800s, tourists and travelers started carving their names on monuments in distant places. There are also examples of graffiti by soldiers. Many young men left a record of their names before they went into battle.

Sign that rock!

In the 1840s, many people traveled west across America hoping to find gold. This race to find riches was called the gold rush. Some people carved their names on the rocks they passed. One boulder in Wyoming is called the Signature Rock because it has so many names carved into it.

The graffiti writers of the 1960s started a trend for writing on trains, such as this subway in New York City.

Spray-paint graffiti

In the 1960s, some people in New York City began using spray paint to create graffiti. They painted **tags** in public places, especially on **subway** trains. Some of them created complete spray-art scenes on long stretches of tunnels and walls.

The new graffiti style spread rapidly. Today you can see examples of spray-can graffiti in most cities of the world.

Some of the names carved into this Greek temple date back to the 1890s. Carving on ancient monuments like this is actually a crime.

Graffiti, Art, and Music

Graffiti has become part of modern **culture**. It has strong links with **hip-hop** and **rap** music. Many modern artists use graffiti styles in their paintings. Designers create fashions that are strongly influenced by street art. There are even computer games about graffiti.

From the street to the gallery

In the 1980s, some graffiti writers began to paint on **canvas** as well as in the streets. Jean-Michel Basquiat and Keith Haring both started out as graffiti artists in New York City. Later, they became leading figures in the art world. Today, many graffiti artists create art on canvas for galleries.

Basquiat's works on canvas kept many elements of graffiti style.

Banksy

One of the best-known graffiti artists is Banksy. He is based in the United Kingdom, but he has also painted in Australia and the United States.

Banksy uses **stencil graffiti** to create striking images. His art can be funny but it often has a serious aim. Some of his paintings deal with difficult questions, such as, "What is the point of war?"

Making stencil graffiti

Some artists create stencil graffiti by cutting a design into a thick piece of paper. They tape the stencil to a surface and spray paint over it. When the stencil is removed, only the cut-out design shows up on the surface.

Banksy created this stencil in London, England, in 2006.

Keith Haring

Keith Haring was influenced by graffiti and comic art. As an art student, he began to draw simple chalk figures in the New York City **subway**. Later, he created **murals**, paintings, and sculptures. They all feature lively, colorful figures.

Keith Haring's figures are easy to recognize. They have large, circular heads and they are surrounded by a lot of short lines. The lines help to express the figures' feelings, like **expression lines** in comics.

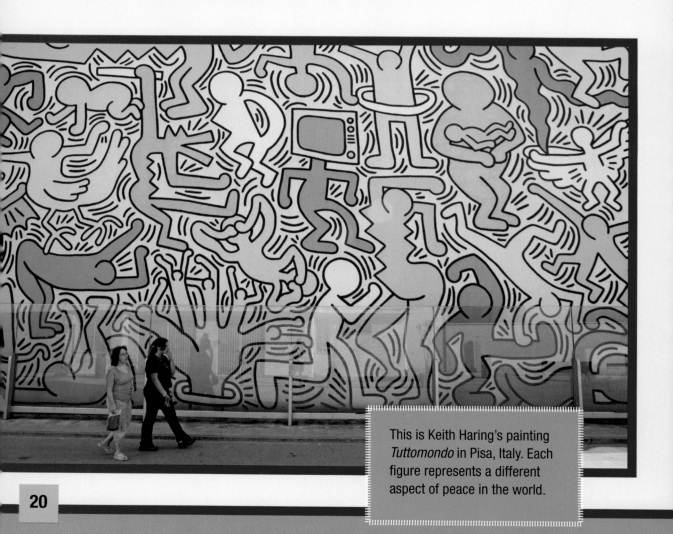

This is Keith Haring's painting *Tuttomondo* in Pisa, Italy. Each figure represents a different aspect of peace in the world.

Figures with feeling

Keith Haring's figures show different emotions through their body shapes. Try using your body to show an emotion. You can work in pairs or larger groups.

Steps to follow:

1. Use your body to **mime** some emotions. Remember a moment when you felt angry or sad, and try to show your feelings through your actions. Make an effort to use all the parts of your body.

2. Choose the emotion you feel you can mime well. Mime the emotion and then freeze like a statue. Get your partner (or the rest of the group) to guess what emotion you are showing.

3. Decide on some good body shapes. Then draw their outlines on a large piece of paper. Work in pairs and take turns. One person can mime the emotion while the other person draws the body shape. Then switch. Keep your figures very simple.

4. Paint your figures with bright colors. Cut them out and stick them to a large piece of poster paper to make a mural. Add expression lines to show the figures' feelings.

Graffiti and hip-hop

Spray-can graffiti, **breakdancing**, and hip-hop music began in New York City in the 1960s. At that time, graffiti writers and rap artists were often members of the same group of friends.

Today, there is still a strong link between hip-hop and graffiti. Graffiti is one of the four elements of hip-hop culture. The other three elements are: rapping, **DJing** (presenting records), and breakdancing. (Look at the book entitled *Hip-Hop* in this series to find out more about the elements of hip-hop.)

Signature tune

Graffiti writers use shapes and colors to create their **tags** or signatures. But have you ever tried to create a signature in sound? In this activity you make up your own signature tune. Then you turn it into a rap.

Steps to follow:

1. First think of a short way to introduce yourself. For example, "I am Abby and I love to dance." Or "Omar's my name and chess is my game!" Clap the rhythm with your hands as you say the words.

2. When you are happy with your introduction, try turning it into a very short rap. The rap should say something about you. It's fun if it rhymes, but it doesn't have to.

3. Try to keep up the rhythm of your rap by clapping your hands or tapping your feet. You could add some dance moves, too.

You could rap together in a group, each taking turns to perform your signature tune.

Hello everybody, I'm called Joe.
When I ride my bike you should see me go!
I kick a ball it goes so far
Anyone can see I'm a superstar!

23

The Problem of Graffiti

Skillful graffiti on legal walls can look great. But when a building is plastered with **tags**, it can look ugly, messy, and depressing. Careless graffiti can ruin the look of homes, stores, and restaurants. It can cause permanent damage to old and beautiful buildings. It can also be extremely expensive to clean up.

It is not surprising that many people think that graffiti should be banned. But what is being done to stop it?

Graffiti and crime?

Some people claim that graffiti encourages crime. They believe that once an area is covered with graffiti, people stop looking after it. Other damage follows, such as broken windows, and soon there are break-ins and thefts. However, not everyone believes that graffiti leads to crime. Some people think that legal graffiti can improve an **urban** environment.

Messy graffiti like this makes an area look ugly and rundown.

24

It's a crime

In most countries, writing graffiti without permission is a crime. People who are caught painting on walls can be given large fines. If they have caused serious damage, they can go to prison for up to 10 years. However, it is not always easy to find the people who do it. **Illegal** graffiti writers can be very hard to track down.

Cleaning up

Most city authorities try to stop graffiti. They run regular cleanup programs and paint buildings with anti-graffiti paint. Often, graffiti writers who have been caught have to join a cleanup team.

A worker uses special chemicals to get rid of graffiti from the side of a train.

What next?

Will street art still be fashionable in 10 years' time? Or will graffiti writers be driven off the streets? Nobody knows what will happen to graffiti, but a few new trends have emerged.

Walls of fame

Some authorities have created spaces where graffiti writers can work legally. These legal walls are sometimes known as "walls of fame" because they give artists a chance to show their work.

Many people hope that legal walls will help solve problems with graffiti. If artists have good spaces where they can express themselves, they may not feel the need to paint **illegally**.

This is part of a wall of fame in Venice Beach, California.

In many places graffiti has become part of the everyday **urban** environment.

Woodblock graffiti

In the last few years, some graffiti writers have started painting on wood. They paint on plywood boards, which they then attach to street signs with metal bolts. This type of street art is known as woodblock graffiti. It displays the writer's skill without damaging buildings or walls.

Clean stencils

Recently, there has been a trend for a new kind of **stencil graffiti**. Artists tape a stencil to a very dirty wall. Then they spray it with a strong cleaning fluid, leaving a clean design on the wall. The only way to remove the stencil is to clean the whole wall!

Timeline

	BCE
c. 60,000	Humans start to paint designs on cave walls.
c. 3300	Picture writing is invented in the Middle East.
c. 3100	Egyptian builders carve graffiti in stone quarries.
c. 3000	The first carvings are made on Graffiti Rock in Saudi Arabia.
c. 1100	The Greeks carve graffiti on their monuments.
c. 750	Roman towns and cities have many examples of carved graffiti.
	CE
c. 200	The Mayans carve graffiti on walls in the city of Tikal, located in modern-day Mexico.
c. 790	Vikings from Scandinavia begin their raids on Europe. They leave examples of carved graffiti.
c. 800	European builders and soldiers carve graffiti on castle and cathedral walls.
c. 1350	Italian artists carve their names on ancient Roman monuments.
1450	Johann Gutenberg invents the printing press in Germany.
c. 1800	Tourism starts to become popular. Early tourists carve their names on monuments.
1848	The California gold rush begins. People carve their names on rocks on the way to California.
1914	World War I begins in Europe and lasts until 1918. Soldiers leave carved records of their names.

1939	World War II begins in Europe and lasts until 1945. American soldiers leave carved and painted graffiti in Europe and the Far East.
1949	American inventor Edward Seymour invents canned spray paint.
1960s	Rival gangs in U.S. cities start painting **tags**. **Hip-hop** begins in New York City.
1970s	Graffiti writers in New York City use spray cans to paint **subway** trains, tunnels, and walls.
1977	Jean-Michel Basquiat starts painting graffiti in New York City.
1980	Keith Haring starts making chalk drawings in the New York City subway.
1981	Graffiti artist Blek le Rat starts creating **stencil graffiti** in Paris, France.
1982	New York City **Rap** Tour visits Paris and London, introducing graffiti and rap to Europe.
1989	The Clean Train Movement begins in New York City. It is one of many campaigns to remove and prevent graffiti.
1992	Banksy starts to paint stencil graffiti.
2008	An exhibition of pieces by Banksy and other stencil artists is held in a disused railway tunnel in London.

Glossary

3-D three dimensional. A 3-D shape has three dimensions (length, width, and depth).

archaeologist someone who learns about the past by uncovering and studying old buildings and objects

breakdancing energetic and acrobatic dancing, involving a lot of moves close to the ground

canvas surface used for painting, made from heavy cloth stretched over a wooden frame

color fade color that slowly fades and changes into another color

communist system of organizing a country so that all the land, houses, and factories belong to the state and all the profits are shared by everyone

culture ways that people express themselves through art, music, dance, writing, and theater

DJing presenting records by mixing and scratching

enclosure place where animals are kept

expression line line that artists use to show feelings

hip-hop culture that began in New York City in the 1960s

illegal against the law

law rules of a country that are made by the government. It is against the law to make graffiti in many places, but in some places it is allowed.

medieval belonging to a period of history between around 1000 and 1450

mime act using movements and actions instead of words

mural wall painting

politician someone involved in governing a country

prehistoric belonging to a time long ago, before history was written down

rap talking with a background of music, using rhythm and rhyme

stencil graffiti paintings made by spraying paint on a card with a shape cut out of it

straights simple capital letters

subway tunnel where trains run in a city

tags short nicknames used by graffiti writers

urban belonging to towns and cities

Find Out More

Books

Harris, Nathaniel. *Wall Paintings* (*Stories in Art*). New York: PowerKids, 2009.

Mack, Jim. *Hip-Hop* (*Culture in Action*). Chicago: Raintree, 2010.

Websites

www.haringkids.com
This brilliant website is based on the art of Keith Haring, and has lots of activities.

www.artofthestate.co.uk/banksy/banksy.htm
This website has over 300 examples of Banksy's pieces.

Places to see graffiti

The places listed below are legal walls where you can see the work of graffiti artists.

Los Angeles, California
The Venice Graffiti Pit, a legal graffiti wall in Venice Beach, is popular with both graffiti artists and tourists.

New York City, New York
The East Harlem Graffiti Wall of Fame at 106th Street and Park Avenue is a world-famous graffiti site that was started in the 1980s and is still being added to today.

Index